Enslow PUBLISHING

BY KATHRYN WALTON

VOL. 1 *From Past to President* 1789

GEORGE WASHINGTON

Please visit our website, www.enslow.com. For a free color catalog of all our high-quality books, call toll free 1-800-398-2504 or fax 1-877-980-4454.

Library of Congress Cataloging-in-Publication Data

Names: Walton, Kathryn, 1993- author.
Title: George Washington / Kathryn Walton.
Description: Buffalo, NY : Enslow Publishing, 2025. | Series: From past to president | Includes index.
Identifiers: LCCN 2024028843 (print) | LCCN 2024028844 (ebook) | ISBN 9781978542402 (library binding) | ISBN 9781978542396 (paperback) | ISBN 9781978542419 (ebook)
Subjects: LCSH: Washington, George, 1732-1799–Juvenile literature. | Presidents–United States–Biography–Juvenile literature.
Classification: LCC E312.66 .W26 2025 (print) | LCC E312.66 (ebook) | DDC 973.4/1092 [B]–dc23/eng/20240802
LC record available at https://lccn.loc.gov/2024028843
LC ebook record available at https://lccn.loc.gov/2024028844

Published in 2025 by
Enslow Publishing
2544 Clinton Street
Buffalo, NY 14224

Copyright © 2025 Enslow Publishing

Portions of this work were originally authored by Gillian Gosman and published as *George Washington*. All new material in this edition is authored by Kathryn Walton.

Designer: Claire Zimmermann
Editor: Natalie Humphrey

Photo credits: Cover (George Washington portrait, signature) courtesy of the Library of Congress; cover (illustrations) Morphart Creation/Shutterstock.com; cover (newspaper clipping) STILLFX/Shutterstock.com; cover (author name scrap), series art (caption background) Robyn Mackenzie/Shutterstock.com; series art (green paper background) OLeksiiTooz/Shutterstock.com; cover (newspaper text background at lower left) MaryValery/Shutterstock.com; series art (newspaper text background) TanyaFox/Shutterstock; series art (More to Learn antique tag) Mega Pixel/Shutterstock.com; pp. 5, 7, 9, 10, 19 (ripped blank newspaper piece) STILLFX/Shutterstock.com; pp. 5, 11, 17 Everett Collection/Shutterstock.com; p. 7 Young_George_Washington.jpg/Wikimedia Commons; p. 9 Washington_1772FXD.jpg/Wikimedia Commons; p. 10 Martha_Custis_Washington_as_a_young_woman_circa_1843_(Steel_engraving).jpg/Wikimedia Commons; p. 13 courtesy of the Metropolitan Museum of Art; p. 15 Foundation_of_the_American_Government_by_Henry_Hintermeister.jpg/Wikimedia Commons; p. 19 Gilbert_Stuart_-_George_Washington_-_Google_Art_Project.jpg/Wikimedia Commons.

All rights reserved. No part of this book may be reproduced in any form without permission in writing from the publisher, except by a reviewer.

Some of the images in this book illustrate individuals who are models. The depictions do not imply actual situations or events.

Printed in the United States of America

CPSIA compliance information: Batch #CWENS25: For further information contact Enslow Publishing at 1-800-398-2504.

CONTENTS

President George Washington 4

Washington's Early Years 6

Joining the Military 8

A Leader 10

The American Revolution 12

Writing the Constitution 14

The First President 16

Stepping Down 18

Remembering Washington 20

President Washington's Timeline 21

Glossary 22

For More Information 23

Index 24

Words in the glossary appear in **bold** type the first time they are used in the text.

PRESIDENT GEORGE WASHINGTON

Being the first to do something can be exciting, but it can also be a lot of hard work! This is what George Washington faced. While he had been a leader in the military, he had no **experience** for the most important job he would take: running a new United States!

Washington set a **precedent** for all the presidents that would follow him. Many of the ideals, morals, and thoughts about what a president should be were started by George Washington.

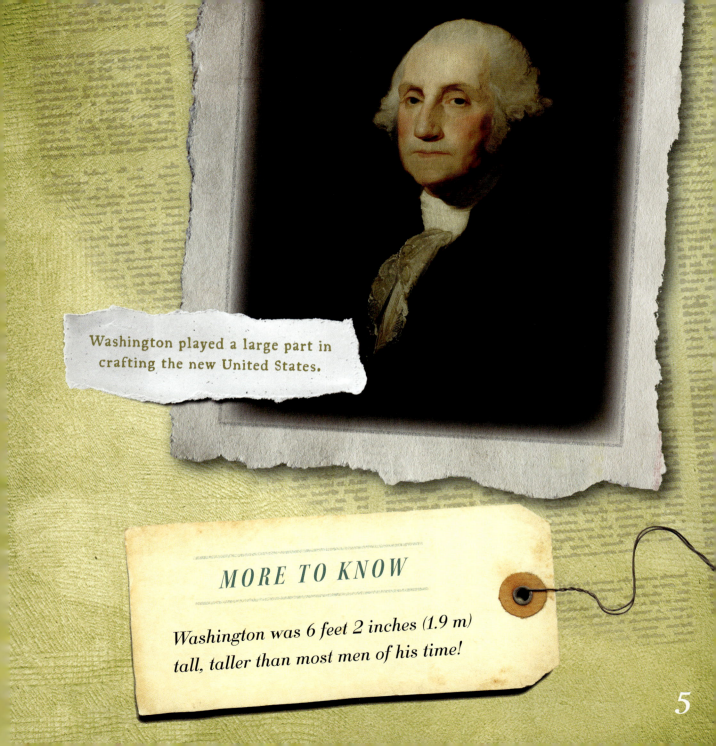

Washington played a large part in crafting the new United States.

MORE TO KNOW

Washington was 6 feet 2 inches (1.9 m) tall, taller than most men of his time!

WASHINGTON'S EARLY YEARS

George Washington was born on February 22, 1732, in Pope's Creek, Virginia. His family owned several large farms. At the time, Virginia was still a British colony. A colony is land owned and controlled by another country.

MORE TO KNOW

George Washington had a big family. He had five siblings and four half siblings!

Washington's father died when Washington was 11 years old. Washington was probably taught by private teachers and went to a local school. He was good at math and geometry.

At 16, Washington joined an **expedition** to make maps of the Shenandoah Valley in western Virginia.

JOINING THE MILITARY

In 1752, Washington joined the British army. He later became an officer. He fought on the side of the British in the **French and Indian War**. Though still a young man, he saw many battles. Washington learned a lot about leading an army and gained important military experience.

MORE TO KNOW

Washington was just 22 years old when he fought in his first battle.

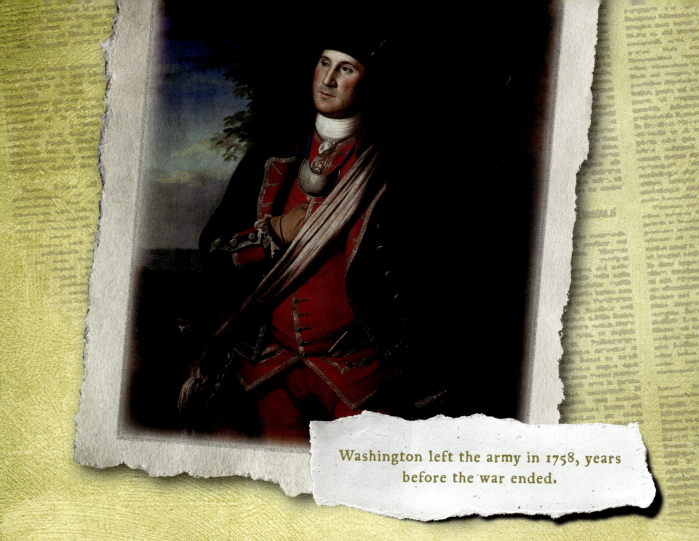

Washington left the army in 1758, years before the war ended.

The war ended in 1763. By this time, many colonists weren't happy. They were beginning to talk about the colonies becoming independent from England.

A LEADER

Washington served in the colony of Virginia's government from 1758 to 1776. In 1774, he was a Virginia **delegate** at the First **Continental Congress**.

In 1775, Washington traveled to Philadelphia, Pennsylvania, as a delegate to the Second Continental Congress. This Congress was the group in charge of the colonies at the start of the American Revolution. The Congress chose Washington as the leader, or commander-in-chief, of the new Continental army.

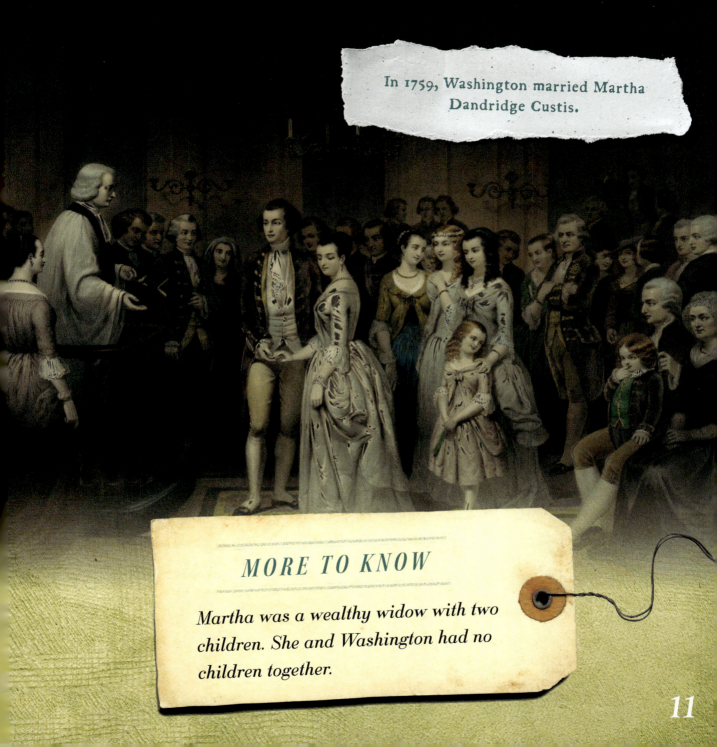

In 1759, Washington married Martha Dandridge Custis.

MORE TO KNOW

Martha was a wealthy widow with two children. She and Washington had no children together.

THE AMERICAN REVOLUTION

In 1775, the American Revolution began. The American Revolution was the war in which the colonies won their freedom from England. Washington and his army won important battles in the New Jersey towns of Trenton, Princeton, and Monmouth.

MORE TO KNOW

During the American Revolution, Washington didn't return home. Instead, his wife Martha would visit him at his military camp.

In 1781, Washington led his men to victory at the Battle of Yorktown, in Virginia. The British surrendered, or officially gave up. England agreed to give the American colonies their independence. The war ended in 1783 with the signing of the Treaty of Paris.

Washington became a military hero for his leadership in the American Revolution.

WRITING THE CONSTITUTION

During the war, the members of the Second Continental Congress wrote the Articles of Confederation. They went into effect in 1777. The Articles were meant to be basic laws the new states needed to follow. But it soon became clear the Articles were not strong enough to guide the new nation.

In 1787, Washington led the Constitutional Convention in Philadelphia. At this meeting, the delegates decided to write a new **document**: the U.S. Constitution!

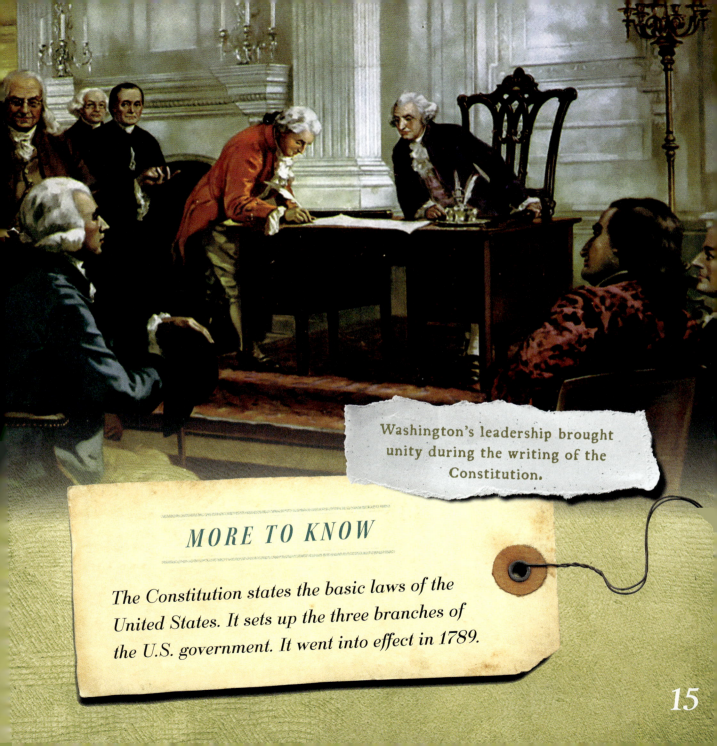

Washington's leadership brought unity during the writing of the Constitution.

MORE TO KNOW

The Constitution states the basic laws of the United States. It sets up the three branches of the U.S. government. It went into effect in 1789.

THE FIRST PRESIDENT

After the states ratified, or approved, the Constitution, it was time to pick a president. Washington was **elected** in 1789. Washington didn't want to lead the new country but still accepted the job.

During Washington's presidency, there were wars going on in Europe. Washington felt it was best for the young United States to be neutral, or to not pick sides in the wars. Instead, he worked to bring the new states together as a strong, safe nation.

Washington's **inauguration** was in New York City.

MORE TO KNOW

Washington had wanted to retire, or stop working, and live the rest of his life on his farm with his family.

STEPPING DOWN

Like many of the presidents that followed him, Washington served two terms as president. His second term ended in 1797. Washington believed that change was important for a **democratic** government. He did not want to become a lifetime ruler, like the kings in Europe.

Washington wrote a farewell letter to the nation when he stepped down as president. He told people to work together. He wanted to keep the young country strong.

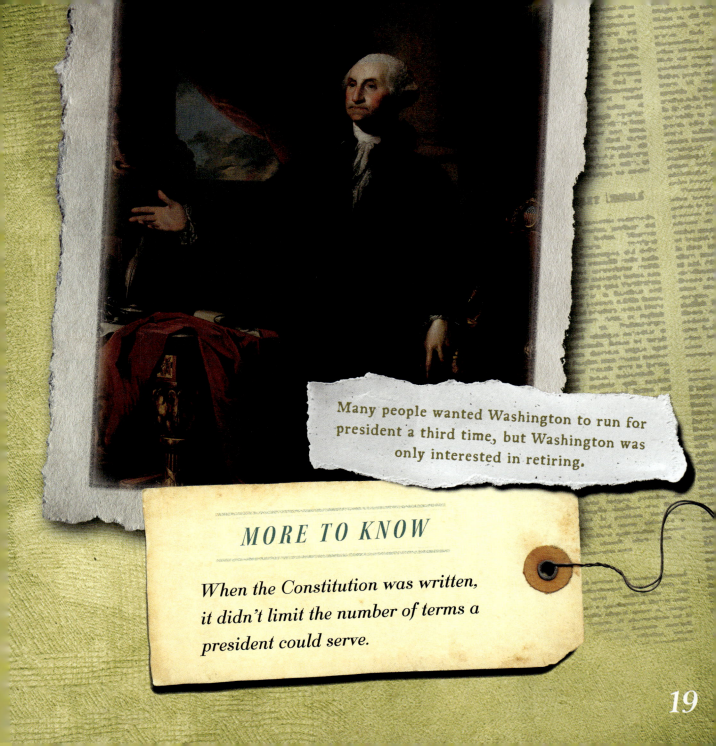

Many people wanted Washington to run for president a third time, but Washington was only interested in retiring.

MORE TO KNOW

When the Constitution was written, it didn't limit the number of terms a president could serve.

REMEMBERING WASHINGTON

After he left office, Washington returned to his home in Virginia to live out the rest of his life. On December 13, 1799, Washington went to bed feeling sick. He died on December 14, 1799.

Washington is remembered as both the first president of the United States and one of the great examples of American democracy. Through his hard work leading the young country, he set an example for what the president should be.

MORE TO KNOW

Washington's home is called Mount Vernon. Many people visit it every year to learn more about Washington's life!

PRESIDENT WASHINGTON'S TIMELINE

FEBRUARY 22, 1732
George Washington is born in Virginia.

1749
Washington begins to make maps of Virginia.

1752
Washington joins the British military.

1758
Washington begins serving in Virginia's government.

JANUARY 6, 1759
Washington marries Martha Dandridge Custis.

1775
Washington becomes the commander-in-chief of the Continental army.

OCTOBER 19, 1781
Washington leads the Continental army in the Battle of Yorktown.

SEPTEMBER 3, 1783
The Treaty of Paris is signed.

1789
Washington becomes the first president of the United States.

1793
Washington begins his second presidential term.

DECEMBER 14, 1799
Washington dies at Mount Vernon.

GLOSSARY

Continental Congress: A meeting of colonial representatives before, during, and after the American Revolution

delegate: A person who is chosen to act for a group.

democratic: Having to do with a form of government in which all citizens take part.

document: A formal piece of writing.

elect: To choose for a position in government.

expedition: A trip made for a certain purpose.

experience: Skill or knowledge gained by doing something.

French and Indian War: The North American part of a larger conflict between England and France called the Seven Years' War.

inauguration: A ceremony marking the start of someone's term in public office.

precedent: Something done or said in the past that sets a model for the future.

FOR MORE INFORMATION

BOOKS

Knopp, Ezra E. *Myths and Facts About George Washington.* Buffalo, NY: PowerKids Press, 2024.

Pettiford, Rebecca. *George Washington.* Minneapolis, MN: Bellwether Media, Inc., 2022.

WEBSITES

Britannica Kids: George Washington
https://kids.britannica.com/kids/article/George-Washington/345536
Learn more about Washington and how he led the new United States.

National Geographic Kids: George Washington
https://kids.nationalgeographic.com/history/article/george-washington
Find out more about George Washington's military life and life as president.

Publisher's note to educators and parents: Our editors have carefully reviewed these websites to ensure that they are suitable for students. Many websites change frequently, however, and we cannot guarantee that a site's future contents will continue to meet our high standards of quality and educational value. Be advised that students should be closely supervised whenever they access the internet.

INDEX

American Revolution, 10, 12, 13

Articles of Confederation, 14

Battle of Yorktown, 13, 21

British army, 8, 21

colonies, 6, 9, 12, 13

Constitutional Convention, 14

Continental army, 10, 12, 21

Custis, Martha Dandridge, 11, 12, 21

death, 20, 21

England, 9, 12, 13

family, 6, 7, 11

First Continental Congress, 10

first presidential term, 16, 21

French and Indian War, 8, 9

inauguration, 16

Philadelphia, Pennsylvania, 10, 14

school, 7

Second Continental Congress, 10, 14

second presidential term, 18, 21

Treaty of Paris, 13, 21

U.S. Constitution, 14, 15, 19

Virginia, 6, 7, 10, 20, 21